Swaziland

Macmillan
Boleswa

First published 1980
New Edition 1993

Published by
Macmillan Boleswa (Pty) Limited
P.O. Box 1235 Manzini Swaziland

Typeset in 11 on 15 pt Souvenir Roman

ISBN 0 333 37182 8

Printed by The Natal Witness Printing and Publishing Company (Pty) Ltd

His Majesty King Mswati III

Acknowledgements

We wish to express our gratitude to the following people for their contributions, help, advice, information, and encouragement in the production of this book.

Albert Chiaranda   *Johnny Masson*
Winston Coetzer   *Dr M. S. Matsebula*
Sipho Dlamini   *Dr S. S. Nxumalo*
Sandra Eastwood   *Vincent Parker*
Pat and Joy Forsyth-Thompson *Dr David Price-Williams*
Martin Forsyth-Thompson *Dirk Schwager*
Zodwa R. Ginindza   *W. P. Stanford*
Austin Hleza   *Wynand van Graan*
Peter McIldowie   *Mark and Liz Ward*
Mduduzi Magongo   *John Wilson*

The publishers are also grateful to the following for permission to reproduce their photographs in this book.

Dirk Schwager: pp 4, 5, 8, 9, 10, 11, 14, 18, 19, 20, 21, 22, 23, 24, 25, 26, 28, 29, 32, 33, 34, 35, 36, 37, 38, 39, 40, 41, 46, 47, 55, 56, 57, 60, 61, 66, 67, 68, 69, 70, 71.

Rod de Vletter: pp v, 1, 2–3, 6–7, 12, 13, 15, 16, 17, 27, 30–1, 42, 43, 44–5, 58, 62, 63, 64, 65, 72.

W. P. Stanford: pp 48–54.

Steve Hall: p iii.

Reed dance.

Contents

Introduction

This book is a visual tribute to Swaziland. In no way does it attempt to be an authoritative work on the history, customs, economy, and geography of Swaziland. Reliable and up-to-date information of this nature is available in the publications given in the bibliography at the end of this book. Our text is a brief summary, which aims at stimulating the reader to discover for himself the excitement and adventure of Swaziland.

While doing background reading on Swaziland we came across the following passage in the obscure memoirs of an early visitor to Swaziland round about the turn of the century.

"Shortly before reaching the Swaziland border we were met by several fine looking warriors. I immediately noted their superiority to other tribes I had known. They were six feet tall, perfectly proportioned and carried themselves with a swinging and dignified gait . . . the women, though in the background, were quite in evidence. Young as I was, I could not help noting that they were the finest looking Africans I had ever seen. These women have perfectly proportioned bodies and stand erect, with their heads thrown back. They are the women of a proud nation and they show it."

We can think of no better introduction to a photographic book on Swaziland. It was definitely the stature and beauty of the Swazis which first prompted us to look more deeply into this surprising and in many ways exquisite country. Since then we have become steadily more entangled in yet another part of mysterious, compelling, sometimes cruel, but also welcoming Africa.

For over three hundred years, the Swazis have been a more or less homogeneous entity. Perhaps this has given them the self-confidence to accept others without fear of losing anything of their own identity. They have a history of peace-seeking. Nevertheless, while establishing themselves in the territory to become Swaziland, certain conflicts were inevitable. The Swazi proved fearless and formidable opponents. Yet they were never vindictive and quickly absorbed the vanquished into the fabric of their own tribal life. This is the background to the racial harmony present in Swaziland today, where equality among equals is a fact. Condescension and servility, the hallmarks of inequality, do not exist in Swaziland. Friendship among races is possible where there is no history of racial prejudice or fear of the other. Pride in one's culture and mutual respect have created this rare and beautiful thing. We dedicate this book to this ideal.

Phophanyane Falls.

Mlumati River.

Gum tree plantations in the Highveld

Timber plantations near Pigg's Peak.

Mbabane from Hospital Hill.

8   Basket stalls at the Mbabane market. This market was founded in the early fifties to give Swazi home industries an outlet and is now a bustling centre for indigenous handicrafts.

Macramé work being done at the Mantenga craft centre in the Ezulwini Valley

Austin Hleza, one of the extremely competent Swazi potters at the Mantenga crafts centre.

Swazi woodcarvers.

Sisal baskets.

14   A typical roadside craftstall selling local wares. This one is one of the many on the road from
Mbabane to Pigg's Peak. The bowls are carved from the indigenous *Mvangati* or Kiat tree.

Shelangubo River.

Participants in the sacred first fruits ceremony, *iNcwala*.

A Swazi warrior at the *iNcwala* ceremony, which takes place between mid-December and mid-January each year.

The annual Reed Dance when all the unmarried girls gather at Ludzidzini royal residence. They collect reeds from various areas in Swaziland for the building of symbolic screens for the Queen Mother's residence. This festival takes place towards the end of August and beginning of September and lasts for three days.

Reed Dance.

20   *Umhlanga.*

Umhlanga.

24   A Swazi princess distinguished by the red feathers of the Purplecrested Lourie in her hair, which
may only be worn by members of the royal family.

A warrior taking part in the Reed Dance.

Men paying elaborate court to the maidens as part of the ritual of the Reed Dance.

Reed Dance.

A Swazi elder and his wife at the Reed Dance

Even the youngest enjoy the Reed Dance.

Nkomazi Valley.

A Swazi warror and his wife dressed in the costume of the sacred first fruits festival, *iNcwala*.

A traditional beehive hut in construction

Top: A fowl's nest plaited into the fabric of a beehive hut.
Bottom: Swazi beehive huts in the Lowveld.

Swazican's fruit canning factory at Malkerns with pineapple fields in the foreground

Grapefruit at Swazican, Malkerns.

As in most African countries, cattle mean wealth. The herds usually consist of Nguni cattle to which
Brahman bulls have been introduced

Some thousands of hectares of maize are being grown in the Malkerns area with the intention of cutting down on imports of this staple food.

40   Tibiyo Taka Ngwane — an organisation which uses mineral royalties as capital — is involved in bee
production, angora goats for mohair production and the development of fish farming. The fish wi
help fulfil the nutritional requirements of the Swazi people as fish have a very high protein value

Tibiyo operates an extensive agricultural programme in the Malkerns Valley. This includes dairy farming, maize and rice production. Tibiyo produces most of the country's milk requirements and is the largest single producer of maize, the staple food of Swaziland. Tibiyo leads in the production of rice and owns the only rice mill in the country.

White rhino in the Mlawula Nature Reserve.

A monitor lizard at Mlawula Nature Reserve.

Malolotja Nature Reserve.

46   Zebra are a common species but still one of the most fascinating and beautiful.
They often herd with the blue wildebeest.

Impala drinking at a dam in the Hlane National Park.

The Plumcoloured Starling (*Cinnyricinclus leucogaster*) is possibly the most beautiful of the starlings in Southern Africa. It is a hole-nester and feeds on fruit, insects and caterpillars.

Purplecrested Lourie (*Tauraco porphyreolopus*). A female with two biggish young nesting about
7 m up in a Knob-thorn (*Acacia nigrescens*), in the Hlane National Park. This is the royal bird of
Swaziland and His Majesty and members of the royal family wear the red wing feathers in their hair.

Top: The Bateleur (*Terathopius ecaudatus*) is one of the most unmistakable eagles of the bushveld
Bottom: A Lizard Buzzard (*Kaupifalco monogrammicus*) photographed high up in a Knob-thorn in
the Swazi bushveld

Top: Whitebacked Vultures (*Gyps africanus*) feeding off the remains of a white rhino carcass. The white streaks on the dead rhino are droppings from the numerous vultures which have perched on it.
Bottom: Marabou Storks (*Beptoptilos crumeniferus*). These storks feed like vultures on carrion. This picture was taken in the Mbuluzi area of the Swaziland bushveld. This was the most southerly nesting place recorded in Southern Africa.

52

Top: A Blackheaded Oriole (*Oriolus larvatus*) feeding in a Tree-fuschia (*Halleria lucida*), which produces vast quantities of nectar
Bottom: The Pygmy Kingfisher (*Ispidina picta*) is the tiniest of our kingfishers. Like the Woodland the Brownhooded and the Striped Kingfishers, which are all dry-land bushveld birds, this little bir does not fish in water but collects insects, spiders and crabs, etc

Top: The Yellowthroated Longclaw (*Macronyx croceus*) — yellowthroated in the Middleveld areas of Swaziland and orangethroated in the Highveld and often considered as two species — is a ground-nesting species.
Bottom: A Purplecrested Lourie.

54   The Scarletchested Sunbird (*Nectarina senegalensis*) is one of the most striking sunbirds of the
Lowveld with its beautiful scarlet chest and green iridescent head and chin. A nectar and insect
eater, it goes for flowers like aloes and the flowering trees of the bushveld.

Top: Swaziland was the home of the San and Khoikhoi peoples for thousands of years before the 55
Nguni migrations of the sixteenth and seventeenth centuries. This is an example of Bushman art,
depicting dancing warriors, from the Nsangwini rock shelters at Pigg's Peak.
Bottom: An extremely rare Bushman painting depicting wildebeest.

The University of Swaziland at Kwaluseni, which was opened by His Majesty, the late King Sobhuza II in 1973.

Top: A section through an excavation of a Middle Stone Age manufacturing site near Ngwenya.
Bottom: Swaziland archaeologists examining ancient soils in the Grand Valley in central Swaziland.

57

Hawane Dam — typical Highveld scenery

59

The Swazi Inn near Mbabane.

The Health and Beauty Centre at the Royal Swazi Spa in the Ezulwini Valley. The spring water is 44 °C where it emerges from the earth.

The casino at the Protea Hotel.

The golf course at the Royal Swazi Sun

Bulandzeni near Pigg's Peak.

The old iron ore mine at Mgwenya has closed down and now forms part of the Malolotja Nature Reserve.

Havelock Asbestos Mine near Pigg's Peak.

Sugar-cane fields near the mill at Big Bend

Sugar production in the Lowveld: the picture at the top shows Mhlume Sugar Mill, while the centre and bottom pictures show operations at the Simunye Mill, which is run by the Royal Swaziland Sugar Corporation.

An aerial view of the irrigation schemes of the Swazi Nation cane farms at Sihhoy

Sunset in the Lowveld.

ACSWAZI – F

iNcwala warriors

Country and Climate

The geography of Swaziland has a textbook-like simplicity. Swaziland divides itself into four clearly defined parallel natural regions running from north to south. Starting in the west these are known as the Highveld, the Middleveld, the Lowveld, and the Lubombo.

The Highveld

This region has a semi-temperate climate. Although fairly high (the average altitude is 1 200 m) it is seldom really cold here, with only an occasional light frost in the winter. The summers are a little humid, with an average rainfall of between 1 000 and 2 250 mm, falling mainly between October and March. The rain in the Highveld is often fairly soft and misty, and lends to these forest regions an atmosphere which is reminiscent of Europe. The moist, earthy, leafy fragrance intensifies this European atmosphere.

The Highveld is rolling, hilly country, gouged dramatically by river gorges. All the major rivers of Swaziland have their sources in the Highveld and flow eastwards towards the Indian Ocean, with an annual discharge of about 9 100 000ℓ per minute (5 000 cusecs).

The two highest mountains are Ngwenya (1 829 m) and Bulembu (1 863 m). Because of the mildness of the Highveld, it was fairly logical to choose Mbabane as the administrative capital of Swaziland even though Manzini in the Middleveld had been the capital of the Swazi nation as long as anyone's oldest ancestors could remember (actually more than 200 years).

The Highveld must originally have been wooded. Primitive agricultural practices denuded much of this region in the last century, but it is now being fairly extensively forested, and boasts some of the largest cultivated forests in Africa.

The Middleveld

If one is driving from Mbabane eastward, one drops down steeply and suddenly finds oneself in the Ezulwini Valley (traditionally known by the Swazis as the Valley of Heaven), and one is well into the Middleveld in twenty minutes. The change in climate and vegetation is just as dramatic as the change in altitude. The forest and short-grassland give way to palm trees, avocados, and bananas. The air is much more humid and the climate generally semi-subtropical. This valley and much of the Middleveld is fairly lush, changing quickly, as the valleys open out, to tall-grassland. Cattle thrive here, so most of the Swazi have always lived here. The royal villages and the legislative centre, Lobamba, are here, as well as Manzini, the commercial and industrial centre. Originally, this region was richly populated by game, and now the beautiful Mlilwane Wildlife Sanctuary preserves this heritage.

The Lowveld

Notorious for malaria in the old days, this is typical sub-tropical "bush" territory. The flat-topped thorn trees and the bright green summer vegetation, which changes to yellow, brown, and ochre in the dry winter, are typical of the bushveld. In the old days, this region was also teaming with impala. The elimination of malaria and subsequent settlement by cattle farmers have greatly reduced the impala herds. Intensive irrigation is making the Lowveld a very promising agricultural region. There is a well-known slogan in Swaziland which says "Sugar serves the nation". Sugar plantations are flourishing and the town of Big Bend has become the lively centre of this development, boasting the presence of three sugar mills.

The Lubombo

This is a sudden, fairly precipitous mountain range, rearing up out of the bushveld. It is the narrowest of the four natural regions and stretches the entire length of Swaziland, separating it from the Indian Ocean coast. The river gorges, known as poorts, which cleave these mountains, contain rare vegetation. Three major rivers run through the Lubombo on their way to the sea, namely the Mbuluzi, the Lusutfu, which is Swaziland's biggest river, and the Ngwavuma. The top of this range has an average altitude of 600 m and the only town in this region is Siteki.
In summer, both the Lowveld and the Lubombo can become uncomfortably hot, often well over 32 °C, but the winters are extremely pleasant.

Swaziland in the Beginning

Nameless oceans advancing and retreating; formless masses of earth rising and sinking; a continent congeals and the forces of nature whittle away at the steaming, cooling, granite collossi.

Countless billions of tiny living organisms, the advance-guard of life, make their mark for an eternity in the crystalline mass of cooling lavas and in the infinite layers of shifting, sifting sands.

Three billion years ago, the granite rocks of Swaziland had come into existence. These are some of the oldest known rocks on earth. Swaziland has become one of the most exciting archaeological fields of the twentieth century. Engraved in the rocks and sediments of Swaziland lies much of the history of mankind, waiting to be read.

One million years ago, a primate, which may well have been an ancestor of Homo Sapiens, the man that thinks, mankind, hunted and was hunted in the mountains of Swaziland. Man himself in the time we know as the Early Stone Age lived and adapted, changed and grew in Swaziland.

Much, much later, coming to terms with an environment often hostile, making tangible efforts to control the world about him, Middle Stone Age man carved tools, made fire, and sheltered in the caves of Swaziland. This period dates from approximately 60 000 years ago. In 1934, Professor Raymond Dart and a team of archaeologists excavated Border Cave in the Lubombo Mountains. After seven years of work, in 1941 they uncovered the skull of a three-month-old Middle Stone Age baby. The skull is estimated to be 48 000 years old. Pear-shaped axe-heads and straight-edged cleavers have been found in astounding quantities, particularly in the terraced gravels of river banks, and revealed in almost perfect chronological order in the layers of soil exposed by soil erosion.

Once man had mastered fire, his relationship with his environment began to take on a new dimension. As in the story of Prometheus, he thought to assume god-like qualities. With heat at his disposal he began to extract ores from the ancient rocks around him. He established his place in the hierarchy of nature. Creation and destruction began to come more easily. In the Ngwenya Hills at Bomvu Ridge, near Oshoek, workings have been found which are carbon-dated to 41 000 BC. This makes it the oldest known mine in the world. The ores, red and black haematite, were at this stage used for colouring body paints and for ritual decoration.

In the Later Stone Age, about 10 000 to 20 000 years ago, the ancestors of the San and Khoikhoi people (popularly known as Bushmen and Hottentots) occupied large tracts of present-day Swaziland. Once again there is a wealth of evidence such as stone implements and rock paintings.

There are twenty known sites of primitive rock paintings. The style of these paintings corresponds with that found in the rest of Southern Africa and is quite definitely Bushman. The paintings depict, with marvellous accuracy of perception, animals common to Swaziland. The eland figures more prominently than the others as it plays an important role in Bushman folklore and tradition. Hunters and dancers are also depicted, but with less accuracy than the animals. A particularly rare painting is one of the blue wildebeest, an animal hardly ever depicted in Bushman rock art. This painting can be seen at Nsangwini. Most of these paintings were discovered by Mr Johnny Masson, a Swazilander who has devoted most of his life to exploring Swaziland.

Sites of great significance have been investigated in Swaziland and exciting additions made to existing theories on the history of man in Africa.

At the time known as the Iron Age, probably about 2 000 years ago, a trickle of people appear to have moved into the country from the north. It is also safe to assume that this was the vanguard of the Bantu-speaking people who occupy much of Southern Africa today.

Iron ore mines at Ngwenya were worked as early as AD 400. Between this time and the true settlement of Swaziland by a homogeneous community, there was desultory tribal settlement. The tribes were almost certainly of Sotho and Nguni origin.

The Story of the Swazi

In a politically unstable world, the success of a benevolent monarchy means good news. King Sobhuza II became the *Ngwenyama* (the Lion) of the Swazi people in 1921. He seemed in many ways to have achieved an impossible goal, that of choosing for his purposes the best of Western culture without destroying the fundamentals of tribal life. He was opposed to the wearing of European dress in the traditional kraals and any bastardisation of what was good in his own Swazi culture.

Swaziland has very vital traditions, amounting to a distinct culture. In present-day Africa, where traditions are generally in a state of radical change, sometimes even moribund, this Swazi culture is an interesting and noble phenomenon. The main reason for this ethnic vitality is that the Swazi are a relatively homogeneous nation.

The Nguni people moved south from Central and East Africa in the fifteenth and sixteenth centuries. In about 1700, these forerunners of the Swazi people, led by Ngwane III, crossed the Lubombo and moved southwards. By 1750 they had settled in the area round the village now known as Hluti. Ngwane died here and was buried in a cave on a hill nearby. His royal male relatives are also buried here, and the cave is still a place of pilgrimage.

Ngwane belonged to the proud Nkosi Dlamini clan, to which the kingship was hereditary. Swazi tradition tells of at least twenty-five kings, but there is certainty only as to the last eight, dating from the late sixteenth century. Ngwane and his successor, Ndvungunye, consolidated their position by absorbing, both by conquest and persuasion, many smaller tribes already in the vicinity. These tribes were of Nguni as well as Sotho origin.

While the basis of the Swazi nation was being laid, Zulu expansion in the south, particularly under the great Shaka, was reverberating far into the present-day Orange Free State and Transvaal.

Sobhuza I, successor to Ndvungunye, expediently moved northwards to the centre of the Middleveld. Today this is the heart of Swaziland. Lobamba is the traditional home of the Queen Mother, and the legislative capital of Swaziland.

The Sotho tribes already living in this area hardly resisted Sobhuza and sooner or later gave allegiance to the Nkosi Dlamini clan, becoming known amongst the Swazis as "These found ahead".

Sobhuza I is known to have been a strategist. He avoided any confrontation he wasn't sure of winning. He also married shrewdly. His main wife was Thandile, daughter of a powerful erstwhile enemy, Ndwandwe. He sent two of his daughters as brides to Shaka and restrained himself from reacting when Shaka murdered them, as Shaka did all his wives when they became pregnant.

The Swazis later encountered the Zulu armies in open battle. Fortunately this happened after Shaka's time, else the outcome might well have changed the course of Swazi history. Shaka was murdered by his half-brother Dingane, who then took over as tyrant of the Zulus. He was even more cruel than Shaka, but without Shaka's military genius. His encounter with the Boers in 1838 broke the power of the Zulu impis. Dingane withdrew into Swaziland with his retinue, where he encountered the Swazis and was finally defeated.

A King's Dream

Sobhuza I, shortly before he died, dreamed a prophetic dream. Up to this point he had had no contact with the White man. It is unlikely that he had even heard of him. In the dream he was told of the coming of pale-skinned people with hair like the tails of cattle. He was warned among other things never to spill the blood of these people, as to do so would be to destroy the Swazi nation. The reason this dream played such an important role in the history of the Swazis is because of the nature of kingship in Swazi society. The king is an embodiment of the nation: his health and fertility relate directly to the nation's prosperity and the fertility of the soil. He is imbued with mystical qualities which give him what could be termed semi-divine status. His utterances have a deep almost mystic significance. Sobhuza's dream seems to have shaped Swazi policy as regards subsequent contact with Whites. The Swazis have never been defeated by Whites because they have never been at war with them. Sobhuza I died shortly after this dream, in 1836, and left to his son Mswati, son of Thandile, a well-established and compact kingdom.

Mswati, Terror of the North

Tribal populations in Southern Africa were increasing, with a lot of land now being taken up by the Whites. This situation led to conflict among the tribes themselves and between the Africans and the Whites. Mswati became the greatest of the Swazi fighting kings. He followed the Zulu pattern in the reorganisation of his regiments by arming them with short stabbing spears as well as the traditional throwing spears. His army's raids reached as far north as what is now Zimbabwe. This Dlamini king continued the policy of absorbing the conquered tribes as long as they recognised and honoured his kingship. The Swazi nation grew, and the additions were of the same tribal stock, that is Nguni, with a sprinkling of Sotho. Many tribes recognised Mswati's power and came to him to be hidden in "his armpit", when being threatened by others.

Mswati had become king at sixteen years of age, in 1840. Four years later he sent messengers to look for missionaries to come to his country. This was also directly as a result of Sobhuza's dream. In it the Whites had come bearing books and metal discs (money). Sobhuza had been told to accept the books and so he had advised his people to accept the teaching of the Bible.

Eventually the Wesleyan Mission in Grahamstown was able to respond to the request, and the Rev. James Allison, the Rev. Richard Giddy, and two Basotho evangelists made their rather adventurous way to Swaziland, where they were warmly received and listened to attentively. The first Christian chapel was built near the village of Dlovunga, with the local Swazi helping in the building and in the planting of a garden.

A small school was built at Mahamba, a little way from the original chapel, and the task of converting Swazis and teaching them to read and write was begun. Allison was also responsible for pioneering the use of siSwati as a written language.

It was during this period, roughly 1845 to 1865, that European settlement in Natal and the Transvaal took place on a large scale. Whites also came to Swaziland, and relationships between Whites and Swazis were always cordial. The fact that the Whites were divided into two definite and increasingly antagonistic groups, namely the British and those of Dutch origin, was later to cause much tension and confusion in and around Swaziland. Doubtful land transactions took place between the Whites and Swazis, which later led to some degree of resentment and ill-feeling on both sides. This was a prelude to one of the hardly creditable and rather undignified land scrambles which took place in Swaziland after the first discovery of gold there in the 1870s.

By the end of Mswati's rule, he had succeeded in uniting all the various clans into a formidable nation. The name *Swazi* is a derivative of Mswati's name, and means the People of Mswati. He died at his home, the royal residence, at Hhohho, in July 1868. He was buried with his father and grandmother at the royal burial hill at Mbilaneni. His death ended the era of Swazi conquest and territorial expansion.

The new king chosen was Ludvonga, and because he was only eleven years old, his uncle, Prince Ndwandwa, acted as regent. Ludvonga died fairly soon afterwards and, as the prince regent was held responsible for his safety, he was put to death. There followed a period of turmoil and confusion, amounting almost to anarchy.

Mswati, in the true tradition of Swazi kings, had many sons, all of whom had an eye on the kingship. Eventually a successor was named. He was Mbandzeni, and he was given the title of Dlamini IV.

A Boer delegation arrived at the coronation ceremony, ostensibly as a courtesy to the new king, but actually to conclude a treaty with the Swazis. The agreement reached was that the Swazis promised to recognise and respect the Boer presence in return for a Boer guarantee to respect Swazi independence and to give them military assistance should they need it. Boers living in Swaziland were also promised protection and freedom of commerce and industry.

This link between the Boers and the Swazis caused some consternation among the British in Natal. Tension between Boer and British was slowly mounting throughout South Africa, and Swaziland constantly found herself a pivot between the two. There are many incidents in this period where either the British or the Boers made use of Swaziland in attaining certain local objectives, the results of which, and the ensuing alleged land deals, were extremely ambiguous.

The Concessions Debacle

The discovery of gold in Swaziland set off a Klondike-like goldrush. Bizarre characters flocked into the country and often exploited Swazi goodwill and gullibility. Many of the problems arising from this period have still not been solved. Land concessions were handed out with gay abandon. Concessions were sold for just about anything under the sun, including things like permission to sell refreshments on the railways. There has never been a passenger railway service in Swaziland. When it was realised that just about the whole of Swaziland had been conceded to foreigners, attempts were made to halt the process and recover some of the land. This resulted in legal wrangles of mind-boggling complexity, which were largely unsuccessful, with again both Boers and British jostling for position. To try to understand why Dlamini IV allowed a situation like this to develop, the renowned Swazi historian, Dr James Matsebula, quotes the following passages. The first one is by A. G. Marwick, a District and later Resident Commissioner of Swaziland extremely familiar with Swazi history.

"In order to understand the Swazi point of view about concessions it is necessary to realise their attitude towards the tenure of land. The private ownership of land was unknown amongst them, and indeed throughout the Bantu world before the advent of the White man.... The land was vested in the whole nation and belonged to the generation also to follow: only the control of the use of it was in the hands of their ruler. Such use might be given to anybody, so long as the land was not needed by the members of the tribe, and it was in the power of the ruler to vary his grant of land and even to cancel them for a good cause arising from the behaviour of the grantees and from the needs of his people."

The second quotation is by Archdeacon Christopher Watts.

"In granting land concessions, Mbandzeni (Dlamini IV) had always been under the impression that he granted the land only for the lifetime of the actual petitioner. The idea of a grant in perpetuity was one quite beyond his comprehension. Mbandzeni understood by granting a land concession that the European could live and graze his cattle on the land undisturbed, but should not have the power to claim it for his own in the sense that he could control it or turn anyone else off.''

Dr Matsebula is justified in maintaining that Swazi law and custom did not recognise the alienation of national assets, and the concessions debacle was one which arose out of total misunderstanding on both sides. As confusion worsened, Dlamini IV, otherwise still known as Mbandzeni, requested the help of a British agent to sort out European interests and to advise him. Britain felt a bit awkward about committing herself, and so in 1886 Dlamini IV appointed Theophilus (''Offy'') Shepstone to the post. It is doubtful if this was the best solution, but at least it was a neutral one as regards the Boer/British situation.

Anglo-Boer Tension over Swaziland

The Boer South African Republic needed an outlet to the sea and the route through Swaziland was the obvious one. Oom Paul Kruger, President of the South African Republic, had long had an eye on Swaziland. In 1895 Britain proclaimed certain parts of Zululand to be administered by Natal. Britain also got together with Boers in the Transvaal long enough to agree to the Boer Republic administering Swaziland.

Swaziland, because of its geographical position, was one of the elements in the struggle that was developing between the British and the Boers. The goldfields on the Witwatersrand were a great source of wealth. Cape Town and Durban were in British hands and President Kruger urgently needed an independent outlet to the sea. The most obvious route lay through Swaziland, to Kosi Bay, south of Portuguese territory.

Cecil Rhodes in the Cape, with his grandiose dreams of expansion towards the north, was instrumental in arranging the bribe which allowed President Kruger the rather arbitrary right of administration over Swaziland in return for allowing Rhodes with his British sympathies to continue his probes into Rhodesia.

This disturbed the Swazis greatly, and they immediately sent off a deputation to England asking to be placed under British protection. The British expressed sympathy and goodwill but did nothing. Although relations between Boer and Swazi had always been cordial, the idea of losing independence was understandably repugnant to the Swazis.

When Britain annexed Tongaland right up to the Portuguese border in 1895, thus sealing off the South African Republic from the sea, Oom Paul began to lose interest in Swaziland.

The Anglo-Boer War broke out in 1899, the year that King Sobhuza II, was born.

The notorious King Bhunu Ngwane V succeeded Mbandzeni, or Dlamini VI, after his death in 1889. During the time that King Bhunu was a minor, his grandmother ruled as regent. After this, his own mother, Gwamile Mdluli, a wise, intelligent woman, could do little other than try to restrain her vicious son. His cruelty and blood-lust made him notorious even within the few short years that he was king. He was actually suffering from terminal tuberculosis, and this made him suspect his enemies of witchcraft against him. The subsequent "smelling out of witches" and the ensuing slaughter were horrific.

King Bhunu's murderous reign had landed him in a precarious legal position with the Boer administrators, but with the outbreak of the Anglo-Boer War, King Bhunu was told to do what he liked and any pretence at administrating Swaziland was abandoned. King Bhunu died; his heir was the infant Sobhuza, the late king of Swaziland. The regency was taken over by his grandmother, Gwamile, and it was with her that the British had to deal after emerging victorious from the war.

A British Protectorate

Swaziland became a protectorate in much the same way as had Basutoland (Lesotho) and Bechuanaland (Botswana). The British assumed this role somewhat reluctantly and pursued a policy of minimal involvement. Britain had acquired guardianship of three territories at a time when she could ill afford any generous development aid, and in addition she was becoming increasingly occupied by the growing tensions in Europe.

The one immediate Swazi problem that was tackled by the new administration was that of the concessions, which had been granted firstly by Mswati and then by Dlamini IV. Most of the deals, apart from the truly ridiculous ones, were ratified by the chief court as being basically legal. The fact that these had occurred as a result of mutual misunderstanding did not detract from their legality. This was a thorny problem and the compromise reached was, briefly, as follows. All concessions for trade and manufacturing were cancelled and paid out. Every valid land claim was properly mapped out, and one-third of the land was handed back to the Swazi nation. This was unacceptable to the Swazis, who again sent a petition to England. Gwamile, that wise old lady the regent, exhorted Swazi men to go to work on the mines on the Rand, to earn money to buy back their land from the Whites. This they did.

During this time, Sobhuza II was growing up and was being prepared for kingship in a way no other king before him had been. He was educated at a local school and as a result of his education he became a Christian, though, wisely, he adhered to no particular denomination. The school he attended was founded by his grandmother and is known as the Zombodze National School. He also attended Lovedale College in the Cape for two years. King Sobhuza was an intelligent pupil, with a pragmatic mind and a great love for books. He was an exceedingly well-informed man and an avid reader.

The Reign of Sobhuza II

In 1921, after three years of ritual training in the traditions of Swazi kingship, Sobhuza was installed as king at the royal kraal at Lobamba. He immediately visited England to pursue the question of the land which his grandfather had allegedly conceded to the Europeans. Even before the Privy Council, his case was unsuccessful. Nevertheless, it was possible by negotiation and the steady buying back of land for Swaziland to resecure more than half the land, which the king holds in trust for the nation — a tenure system common to most African countries.

Colonial rule was not always easy for the Swazis to accept. But it was during this period that the slow movement from a purely pastoral economy to industrial employment and the development of a middle class took place. Sobhuza II showed great patience and circumspection throughout. Towards the end of the '50s the Swazi National Council, under the constant guidance of Sobhuza, began to negotiate for powers beyond those confined to Swazi customs. The British were not insensitive to these stirrings and in 1960 the first steps towards total self-government were made.

Sobhuza II formulated his idea in a historic address to a small but influential group of Swazi and European citizens on the 4th April 1960, and he suggested the formation of a legislative council.

This was the beginning of formal politics in Swaziland. A trade union was formed in response to this speech, and political parties came into being. In 1964 a plebiscite was held, which showed almost total support for the old Swazi National Council. Legislative elections were held and the Mbokodvo National Movement obtained large majorities. The Mbokodvo (which means "grinding stone" in siSwati) policy is to ensure the political expression of the nation's unity under the kingship, the maintaining of traditional conservatism, and the rejection of any semblance of racial discrimination.

After this, independence was negotiated, and on the 6th September 1968 Swaziland became a sovereign state once more.

Constitutional problems continued after independence. A traditional African society cannot simply become an ideal Western-type democracy. A compromise must be made which takes into account traditional infrastructure and decision-making processes. Something new must be created — a system of government which safeguards what is of value in the tradition and culture of the country, but which reflects the new face of Africa.

King Sobhuza II was the ideal man to do this. His greatest gift was his ability to keep a foot in both worlds. He never lost touch with the Swaziland of his forefathers, but was shrewd enough to understand the politics of emergent Africa and to steer a truly magnificent path between extremes. In 1972 he repealed the constitution, except for the judiciary, which he insisted must remain independent. He called on groups of tribal elders to give voice to the people in a traditional way, as to what they wanted to retain in the constitution and what important tribal traditions should be included. Elders travelled abroad to study other constitutions and returned with generally pro-Western sympathies. Steady progress was being made in a uniquely tribal democracy, and new elections, to ratify a new, yet old, truly Swazi constitution, were held in 1978 under the Tinkhundla system.

On the 21st August 1982, His Majesty King Sobhuza II passed away at Embo State House. Her Royal Majesty Indlovukazi Dzeliwe became head of state until August 1983, when she was replaced by Her Royal Majesty Indlovukazi Ntombi (of the Tfwala clan), mother of King Mswati III.

King Mswati III

King Mswati III was born on the 19th April 1968 in Manzini. He was given the name "Makhosetive", which means "King of all nations", by his father King Sobhuza II. The young Prince Makhosetive attended Masundvwini Primary School and Lozitha Palace School. In January 1983 at the age of 15 he left Swaziland to attend school in England, travelling between the two countries for three years, until just before his coronation in 1986. After the death of his father, Prince Makhosetive was officially introduced as Umntfwana, the Crown Prince, on 12th September 1983. His coronation took place on the 25th April 1986, when he was crowned King Mswati III. He was named after King Mswati II — the greatest of the fighting Swazi kings. The coronation was a bright and colourful ceremony which took place over a period of three days. There was dancing by the different regiments of the nation, and heads of state and special representatives came from all over Africa and the rest of the world to witness the occasion.

Since his coronation, King Mswati has had the opportunity to visit many parts of the world. In 1990 he addressed the United Nations General Assembly in New York. He has also participated in many important events for the Southern African region. For example, in 1991 he was appointed Chairman of the Preferential Trade Area (PTA) and this position gave him the opportunity to address the European Economic Community (EEC) on behalf of the African members of the PTA. As the youngest reigning monarch in the world, King Mswati III has to be both a traditional ruler and a modern-day leader, and just as his great and beloved father, King Sobhuza II, led Swaziland into the twentieth century, so will King Mswati III lead his country into the twenty-first century.

Some Swazi Customs

Royal Succession

The Swazi rules for choosing a king are of such simplicity and yet deep-seated wisdom that strife or war over the matter of who the new king is to be is virtually unknown. The king never really knows who his heir is going to be. After his death, the Royal Council chooses the heir from among his children, and this child's mother has to be of impeccable heritage. Usually, but not necessarily, he is the first son of the first wife. Should the Queen Mother be alive, she will automatically become regent until the young crown prince comes of age. The role of the Queen Mother as adviser and co-ruler is extremely important. The royal family of Swaziland, the Dlaminis, do not intermarry, so the king is always a Dlamini and the Queen Mother never a Dlamini. This provides an excellent balance of power between the Dlaminis and the other noble families.

The Swazi King

The status of the *Ngwenyama* (the Lion) of Swaziland has great mystical significance over and above his traditional role of paramount chief, head of the administration, and constitutional monarch. The king is the embodiment of the nation. The health of the king reflects the nation's prosperity. His fertility is a direct reflection of the fertility of the nation's soil. The king is bound to have many wives and children. The nation expects it of him.

The *iNcwala* or Annual Ceremony of Kingship

The writer Hilda Kuper talks about this ritual as having been variously interpreted as: a first fruit ceremony, a pageant of Swazi history, a drama of a kingship, and a ritual of rebellion. This beautiful and complex ceremony is described and analysed in detail in her book *An African Aristocracy*. Here is a brief description of the ritual. The *iNcwala* is a sacred period and lasts approximately three weeks. It is divided into the Little *iNcwala*, which lasts two days, beginning when the sun reaches its summer solstice and the moon is dark, and the Big *iNcwala*, which lasts six days from the night of the full moon.

Between these two there are ceremonial dances in the villages. Special messengers are sent out to collect secret herbs, and water from the main rivers and from the sea. The *iNcwala* reflects the growth of the king and is not a static ritual. When a king has reached full maturity, the *iNcwala* reaches its peak. The honour of opening the *iNcwala* is reserved for the oldest regiment. Other participants all join in, taking their places according to rank and sex. The main rites all take place in secret in the king's sanctuary. A pitch-black ox is slaughtered and the king doctored with parts of its body. At a certain moment a cry is given that the king has broken with the old year and is welcoming the new and a great sacred song is sung in praise of the king "Our Bull". This is the beginning of the Little *iNcwala* and takes place on the darkest night before the moon begins to wax. While the people wait for the moon to grow full, there is preparation throughout the country. The people practise songs and dances for the main ceremony and prepare their ritual costumes of feathers, leopard skins, and cattle-tail cloaks.

On the day of the full moon, a regiment of pure young warriors fetch a sacred tree. The warriors are considered pure if they have had no affairs with married women or made any young girls pregnant. It is said that branches of the sacred tree, a type of acacia which grows only in a few places in Swaziland, will wither if the youth who bears it has transgressed against these rules of purity. All these proceedings are accompanied by dances of the regiments, led by the king.

On the third day of the Big *iNcwala*, the young men of the regiments, dressed only in loin-cloths, chase a black bull into the royal kraal and throw it, and it is ritually slaughtered. The king then sits naked on the black bull and is washed with the sacred water and herbs which have been brought. This renews his virility.

The fourth day is the great day when the king walks naked through his people to the hut where his first ritual marriage took place. There he eats the first fruits of the new season. Now all the people, dressed in their finest clothes, assemble in the royal residence. The Queen Mother, dressed in a leopard-skin cloak, now takes a leading part in the ritual, and there is much dancing and singing. The king, anointed with black medicines, his body covered in green grass, his head-dress of black plumes and with his belt of silver monkey skins, dances the main dances. These dances are improvised as the warriors before him beat out the rhythms on their shields. That night the king sleeps with his first ritual queen and stays in seclusion the next day.

The *iNcwala* ends on the sixth day after the full moon with a ritual cleansing. All the household implements, the king's bedding and clothes discarded in the previous year, together with the remains of the slaughtered bull, are piled onto a bonfire into which the king thrusts a burning stick. A black cow is slaughtered for this part of the ceremony and her gall mixed with the medicated waters with which the king had cleansed himself from all the ritual medicines of the *iNcwala*. The ancient belief is that a rainstorm will come to put out the bonfire. Strangely enough, an *iNcwala* ceremony has seldom passed where this has not happened. The Swazis are known among all the tribes of Southern Africa as great rainmakers. The end of the *iNcwala* is marked by feasting and singing throughout the land.

The *iNcwala*, being a sacred ceremony, is one in which outside participation is not encouraged, and certain parts are strictly secret. On no account may these proceedings be filmed, and only certain parts may be photographed. King Sobhuza II once remarked, ''There are no spectators at the *iNcwala*.''

The Reed Dance or *Umhlanga*

This is not a sacred ceremony, and takes place at the end of August. In this ceremony, the Swazi maidens show respect for the Queen Mother by bringing reeds from all over Swaziland for the building of the symbolic screens round the Queen Mother's residence. This tends to be a strictly feminine occasion where the girls who have remained chaste demonstrate their nubility. The dance climaxes when the girls, dressed in beautiful anklets, bracelets, necklaces, and bead skirts, bring their reeds to the Queen's residence and do a slow dance, in perfect time, past the entrance of the royal village to the cattle kraal behind. On the final day, the girls dance for the Queen Mother, and the festival ends with feasting and rejoicing. Visitors are welcome to attend the *Umhlanga* or Reed Dance.

Sibhaca Dancing

This is the everyday rhythmic, vigorous dancing loved and practised by all Swazis. It has sometimes been referred to as their national sport. King Sobhuza was a great protagonist of the *sibhaca* and a gifted exponent of the dance in his younger days. An annual *sibhaca* competition is held for the king at Entfonjeni, in the Mlumati Valley, where a very high standard of dancing is expected. The *sibhaca* dancers wear colourful costumes of skirts and cow tails round their wrists and ankles. Various teams compete with one another, and visitors are welcome to watch.

MACSWAZI – G

Tourist Attractions

The tourist possibilities in Swaziland are rich and varied, and can be roughly divided into four categories:

- wildlife, nature reserves, and lodges
- hotels, casinos, and spa
- traditional attractions
- sport and adventure.

Wildlife, Nature Reserves, and Lodges

The countryside in Swaziland is so splendid and full of lovely surprises that it is difficult to know where to start. The Highveld, where all the rivers have their sources, is rugged and scenic. The rivers are also free of bilharzia, except for lower down towards the Lowveld. In their passage from Highveld to Lowveld, these rivers afford many splendid waterfalls. The most spectacular ones are found in the Malolotja and Phophonyane Nature Reserves. The walks to these waterfalls are superb and the swimming a sheer delight.

The drive from Mbabane to Pigg's Peak is a scenic wonder. The Pigg's Peak area is also renowned for its handicrafts, especially the original wood and stone carvings and high quality weaving works. More specific and detailed information on drives, walks, and other interesting scenic attractions can be obtained from the Mbabane Tourist Office. The wildlife of Swaziland is very accessible, with most of the parks situated just off the main routes.

Hlane

This is a bushveld reserve in the Lowveld, proclaimed in 1967 by King Sobhuza himself, who was a concerned conservationist. It is approximately 30 000 hectares in size, with 10 500 hectares as the proclaimed nucleus and 19 500 hectares utilised for seasonal dispersal.

Hlane consists of predominantly acacia-dominated savanna with some outstanding stands of Knob-thorn or *Acacia nigrescens*. It is classic big-game country, and this feeling has been enhanced by the reintroduction of elephant to the reserve.

Hlane also plays an important traditional role as it is the venue of the *Butimba* or National Hunt, in which the king plays a predominant part. Before the establishment of Hlane and the special zoning of an area for the hunt adjacent to the proclaimed park, this traditional event had lost much of its significance because of the severe depletion of game.

Mlilwane

Swaziland's first wildlife sanctuary, Mlilwane, was officially opened in 1964 and has grown more than ten times its original size to its present 4 500 hectares. Created and developed through the perseverance of Ted and Liz Reilly and supported by international wildlife organisations, Mlilwane is now haven to a wide variety of animals and birds, many of whom have become used to the presence of man.

The park is bordered in the north by rocky mountains which include the famous Sheba's Breasts and Execution Rock. King Bhunu, the predecessor of King Sobhuza II, was the last king to have actually used Execution Rock for the purpose suggested by its name.

A walking trail has recently been developed in the park, and a network of roads ensures good game viewing and excellent views over the Ezulwini Valley.

Gilbert Reynolds Memorial Garden

This is a really outstanding aloe garden. The late Mr Reynolds, a noted authority on aloes, made this collection, which includes 230 species of aloe from all over Africa and Madagascar, but chiefly from Southern Africa. Aloes are at their best in winter, so this would be the time to visit this garden, which is part of the Mlilwane Sanctuary.

Malolotja

This park, run by the Swaziland National Trust Commission, is situated in the Highveld, along the Transvaal border. It may well be one of the world's most beautiful and rewarding mountain parks. It includes two major rivers, the Nkomazi and the Malolotja, and a truly splendid terrain, comprising rocky mountains, river gorges, swamps, forests, waterfalls, rapids, and fern-fringed pools. The Malolotja Falls, the highest in Swaziland, are over 95 m high.

Another outstanding feature of Malolotja is the mountain flowers. In midsummer the rolling hills and valleys become a vast unruly display of colours as hundreds of species of mountain flowers, many of them rare, blossom in the brilliant sun.

Malolotja is primarily a hiking reserve, and there are over 200 km of walking trails of varying degrees of difficulty. A sense of wilderness is maintained in this area by the authorities who only allow one group of backpackers at a time to stay at any one of the 17 backpacking sites.

An environmental education centre has been established at Malolotja, and much work is being done through this facility to spread environmental awareness to the Swazi nation, with special emphasis on the youth.

Mlawula

Also run by the Swaziland National Trust Commission, this splendid wilderness area is situated in the rugged country of the Lubombo Mountains, in the north east of Swaziland, bordering Mozambique. The park is 18 000 hectares in extent and contains very interesting forests and thickets that are home to rare animals and plants, including three cycad species.

Mlawula has a wide variety of game as well as over 300 species of birds. There is a "vulture restaurant", where visitors can arrange to watch the feeding vultures from a hide.

Some excellent hiking is available in Mlawula, although the hiking trail network is not as extensively developed as that of Malolotja.

Mkhaya

Mkhaya is the nation's special refuge for endangered species. Like Mlilwane, its success can be attributed to Ted and Liz Reilly and the support they have received from wildlife organisations.

Mkhaya is unique in that among the endangered species it protects is the Nguni cow, now highly prized for its hardiness and its resistance to disease. Plains game co-exists with Nguni cattle in Mkhaya in a way reminiscent of the precolonial era.

Numerous species of traditional big game can be found at Mkhaya, notably black and white rhino, and elephant. Other species include tssessebe and roan antelope.

Mkhaya also preserves excellent stands of primeval riverine forest and a variety of other habitats which ensure an excellent diversity of birdlife.

Phophonyane

Phophonyane is the smallest of Swaziland's nature reserves but conserves a valuable area, which includes the series of falls and cascades that make up the Phophonyane Falls. Phophonyane contains some of the lushest riverine habitat to be found in Southern Africa. It is a wonderland of rushing water, riotous vegetation, and abundant birdlife, with spectacular views of the Gobolondlo Mountain range and the Mlumati Valley.

Phophonyane is a privately-owned reserve run by Eco-Africa Safaris. The emphasis in this reserve is on the preservation of habitat. Great effort is required to maintain this area in its natural state as Middleveld areas such as Phophonyane are most prone to invasion from exotic species. If uncontrolled, the foreign plants will totally alter the habitat within a few years.

Muti-Muti

Swaziland's newest conservation area is located just south of Siteki along some cliffs and valleys of the Lubombo range. Differing in habitat from its northern cousin, Mlawula, it also preserves much precious flora in its moistbelt forests and rocky plateaux.

Like Phophonyane it is owned and managed by Eco-Africa Safaris. It has remnant populations of small game and its potential for carrying bigger game is excellent. However, for the present time, emphasis is on birdwatching and hiking through spectacular scenery. From one vantage point in the reserve one can see east over almost the entire area of Swaziland, and across the Mozambican floodplains as far as Maputo.

Hotels, Casinos, and Spa

One of the attractions of Swaziland lies in the convenient availability to the tourist of two quite different kinds of holiday entertainment — the highly sophisticated pleasures of the casinos, such as roulette and blackjack, and the simpler pleasures of the outdoors, such as walking, birdwatching and game-viewing. The casinos at the Royal Swazi Sun, the Pigg's Peak Protea Hotel and the Nhlangano Sun Hotel are pulsating, chic, cosmopolitan gaming centres. They cater for nearly all the major "games of chance" and have private salons for really serious players. The accommodation offered by the casinos and adjoining hotels is also renowned for providing ideal facilities for children, so family stays are fun for all.

Apart from the big casino hotels just mentioned, there are a variety of family-type hotels and lodges dotted around the country. The most popular tourism areas are the Ezulwini Valley and the Pigg's Peak area.

The Ezulwini area is the oldest and most established and has the most to offer in terms of hotels, restaurants, nightclubs and handicraft centres. It is also the location for the aptly named "cuddle puddle", which is a mineral spring emerging from the earth at about 44 °C. This spring is the property of the Royal Swazi Sun and has been developed into a spectacular health and beauty centre. The mineral content of the spring is extremely high and the waters particularly beneficial.

The Pigg's Peak area has become popular for the quality of accommodation that can be found there as well as its magnificent scenery and its proximity to the natural wonders of the Eastern Transvaal.

Traditional Attractions

One starts enjoying traditional attractions in Mbabane, the capital. Here is one of the most authentic and colourful African markets imaginable. This market was started in 1950 to provide Swazi housewives with an outlet for cottage industry products. The money was sorely needed, and these simple crafts have always been of extremely good quality. Grass mats, wooden bowls, shields, spears, knobkerries, walking sticks, and baskets are made at home and brought to the market. Though fairly small, it is packed with individual stalls vibrating with happy, singing, shouting vendors. The baskets are particularly exciting. The workmanship, shapes, and materials make them items of outstanding value, both decoratively and practically. The well-known Swazi bowls, carved out of *Mvang-ati* or Kiaat wood (*Pterocarpus angolensis*), are also outstanding value for money at the market. These beautiful bowls are ideal for salad and fruit, and a variety of shapes and sizes is available. These bowls and original wood and soapstone sculptures are most readily found along the Pigg's Peak road in the Nkomazi River area.

The handicraft industry has grown rapidly in Swaziland and a wide variety of quality handmade goods is available. These range from sophisticated glassware and original-design candles to mohair weaving, cotton prints, and pottery. Shops are found throughout the country, but the industry is centred in the Ezulwini Valley and Malkerns area.

Throughout Swaziland it is common to see Swazi people wearing national dress. This is a colourful way of coping with the heat in summer, and consists of a "kilt" (*emajobo*) of skins and a bright printed cotton *mahiya* worn casually over the shoulders. Traditional necklaces, bracelets, and anklets are worn, and vary according to family, marital status, and gender. It is not unusual to see this cos-tume brightening up even the most serious boardrooms. At hotels where formal Western dress is required at certain times, Swazi national dress is always accept-able.

Sport and Adventure

Sporting facilities and possibilities for adventure are readily available in Swazi-land. The sportsman or woman will find facilities at most of the hotels. Private clubs also allow non-members to participate by signing them on as guests.

Riding facilities are abundant, which is not surprising in a country so eminently suited to this pleasurable pastime. Game viewing on horseback is available in Mlilwane, while other stables offer rides in the rolling grasslands of the Highveld, or through misty pine forests.

Swaziland has numerous golf courses, many of which are found in spectacular settings. Some of these courses are really for the adventurous golfer seeking new challenges. A golf course of international standard can be found in the Royal Swazi Sun's international championship course. Here one may enjoy 18 holes on a well-tended course surrounded by the most breathtaking scenery.

Mountain biking is catered for through a series of trails starting in the Phopho-nyane Nature Reserve, where one can cycle for a whole day in beautiful sur-roundings without meeting another soul.

Birds of Swaziland

Birdwatching in Swaziland

Swaziland is full of surprises for the keen birdwatcher. It is not widely known that Swaziland contains more bird species than the Kruger National Park, which is larger than Swaziland and a very popular venue for birdwatching. In fact, Swaziland contains almost as many species as Botswana, which is about 40 times the size of Swaziland.

The impressive diversity of birdlife in Swaziland is a consequence of the great diversity of habitat which occurs within a small area. The cool, misty Highveld in the west, the thorny plains of the Lowveld, the various transitional habitat types of the Middleveld, and the strange Lubombo Mountains in the east each have their own very different selection of bird species. Moreover, Swaziland's high rainfall (high by Southern African standards) ensures that each of these regions contains significant patches of natural forest.

Top of the list of special birds to be found in Swaziland is the rare and beautiful Blue Swallow. Although endangered by the transformation of much of its montane grassland habitat to pine plantations, these birds can still be seen skimming low over the grasstops of Malolotja. They may also be encountered in a few other grassland areas near Mbabane.

Also of special interest is the nesting colony of Marabou Storks at Hlane, believed to be the only breeding colony south of the Limpopo River. (Although this species is frequently seen in the Kruger National Park, the birds do not breed there.)

There is no bird species which is completely confined to Swaziland, but the Pink-throated Twinspot comes closest to this distinction. This colourful little bird is found in riverine thickets and forest verges throughout the eastern half of the country, and will usually be seen hopping about on or close to the ground. Beyond the borders of Swaziland, this species can be found only in a small area in northern Natal and southern Mozambique.

Of great importance in Swazi tradition is the Purplecrested Lourie. The local name, *Gwalagwala*, describes the raucous call of the bird, which can be heard from dense woodlands in all but the highest parts of the country. Because the scarlet underwing feathers are used to adorn the heads of members of the royal family, this lourie is regarded as the royal bird; the more feathers used, the higher the wearer's rank in Swazi royalty. Anyone other than members of the royal family found killing this bird is liable to severe punishment.

Swaziland's nature reserves all offer excellent opportunities for birdwatching, especially as most of them allow extensive exploration on foot.

Malolotja is an excellent venue for spotting most of the Highveld species. The higher grassland areas have Blue Cranes, Stanley Bustards, Blackwinged

Plovers, Bald Ibis, as well as the Blue Swallow, and in the summer months several species of widows provide a very colourful display. While these grasslands are easily accessible by road, one has to take to the footpaths to explore the forests which occur in the valleys. Here a patient search may be rewarded with spectacular birds such as the Narina Trogon, Knysna Lourie, Chorister Robin, Starred Robin and Green Twinspot.

For those species which occur only in the drier southern Highveld, a visit to the Mhlosheni region is recommended. Here one might look for the Whitebellied Korhaan, Redcapped Lark, and Grass Owl, amongst others.

The most important feature of the Middleveld as far as birdwatching is concerned is the unusual Middleveld forests found most extensively in the north east of Swaziland, near Pigg's Peak. A visit to the Phophonyane Nature Reserve and Mlumati Valley gives one an opportunity to visit these forests and search for the Yellow-streaked Bulbul, Brown Robin, Olive Sunbird, and Yellowspotted Nicator, as well as many of the forest birds of the Highveld.

The thorn savannas of the Lowveld represent perhaps the most rewarding birdwatching habitat of all. This habitat covers much of Africa and typifies what is referred to as the "African bush". It is the sweet, nutritious grasses of these savannas that support the vast game herds of Africa. There is a corresponding wealth of birdlife, and many of the birds of this habitat are large and brightly coloured, such as the hornbills, rollers, and glossy starlings. Moreover the openness of the habitat ensures that they are easy to spot.

The Mlawula Nature Reserve offers good opportunities to see most of the Lowveld birds, as well as the chance to explore the northern part of the Lubombo range. Forested gorges in the Lubombos contain some species typical of the coastal forests to the east, such as the Grey Sunbird, African Broadbill, and White-eared Barbet. In addition, the Mlawula River is a particularly good venue for rare and elusive waterside birds, such as the Whitebacked Night Heron, African Finfoot, and Green Sandpiper.

The southern part of the Lowveld supports a drier and more open thorn savanna, and some of the species more prevalent here include the Lilacbreasted Roller, Brownheaded Parrot, and Longtailed Shrike. The irrigation dams in this area sometimes attract spectacular flocks of waterbirds, including several species of ducks, herons, egrets, storks, pelicans, and flamingoes.

Although nature reserves are the most popular birdwatching venues, there are many exciting birds to look at wherever you might find yourself in Swaziland.

Vincent Parker

Bird Photography in Swaziland

Sitting in the quiet of the bush, hidden from the life going on around me, is fascinating. This is the best therapy for living in the mad, mad world I know; and slowly discovering the personality of "your" bird is enthralling.

The equipment I use is, firstly, a 35 mm camera, and then lenses ranging from 135 mm to 400 mm, and a large zoom (200–600 mm). This zoom can be used for small birds, like the sunbirds, as well as big birds like eagles, storks, vultures, and secretary birds. It is invaluable for photographing birds, and makes much simpler the problems of good composition, good "framing" of the bird, and adjusting to the different sizes of birds from the fixed position of your hide.

The hide itself varies largely depending on what types of birds one is interested in. For species that nest on the ground one obviously needs very low and simple hides, whereas for those nesting high in trees one will need hides of up to 7,5 m high. It is possible to obtain a collapsible aluminium construction, which one covers with camouflage canvas, and which one can adjust to the desired height. In the Highveld, birds like robins, longclaws, sunbirds, etc. nest low down, while in the Lowveld, except for some grass workers and hole nesters, all birds nest high up. A few examples of nest heights are: the Cardinal Woodpecker, 3 m; Redbilled Woodhoopoe, 4,5 m; Black Tit, 2,5 m; Whitebacked Vulture, 15 m; Bateleur, 10 m; Goldentailed Woodpecker, 3 m; and the Marabou Stork, anything from 4 to 25 m. For these nests one needs scaffolding, with platforms to support one's hide at the correct height. If the scaffolding is camouflaged with branches and grass, birds will take quite well to them. Flash bulbs, strangely enough, do not seem to disturb birds unduly.

Two of the most important requirements for bird-photography, however, are time and patience. The birds have to become accustomed to the presence of the hide before one can start moving closer in to the nest or the favourite feeding ground. One can lure the birds, too, if one knows their favourite foods, by putting out maize-meal porridge, small grain, some meat, or small dead vermin for carrion-eaters and birds of prey. Nectar-drinking birds can always be tempted to stay round certain blooms longer if one provides some extra nectar-laden flowers in strategic positions. (A mixture of sugar and water can be injected into these flowers to make them really enticing.) Fruit, of course, is often a good lure, and I have even used honey and beeswax to good effect when photographing honey-guides.

The cardinal rule for all bird photography is never to destroy the nest, either by direct action or by attracting predators by carelessly revealing the presence of the nest. Certain birds, such as bulbuls, longclaws, and even large ones like the Bateleur will desert the nest and even their young if carelessly and inconsiderately approached. My experience of birds in Swaziland is that they have taken very well to certain objects being inserted into their nesting areas as long as respect and good camouflage have been employed.

I photographed the royal bird of Swaziland, the Purplecrested Lourie, in a Knobthorn Acacia about 7 m up. The nest contained two well-grown youngsters which the mother fed frequently by regurgitating fruit and pips. The male, on the other hand, was extremely shy of coming in, and only much later did he join his mate in the nest and allow me to get a picture of them together. The same pattern emerged in my photographing of the Bateleur. The female soon got used to me. When we found the nest, one of the game guards at the Hlane National Park was persuaded to climb up and inspect it. He did this with some trepidation, but imagine my excitement when he reported the presence of two well-grown young. The eagle justified the man's apprehensions by sweeping down threateningly while he was in the tree, but she never attacked. Once I had got myself set up in the hide, all was peaceful again, with the male perched on a tree some 200 m away. He flew in once, carrying a snake about 2,5 m long, but veered away some 3 m from the nest.

Leadwood trees with their hard wood and holes provide many nests for birds in the bushveld. These trees are reputed to be the oldest in the Lowveld, and one in Hlane was carbon-dated by the CSIR (Council for Scientific and Industrial Research) in South Africa as being about 1 041 years old. It had died about 147 years ago, and so this Leadwood was growing in Hlane some 100 years before William the Conqueror landed in England. This wood is known by the Swazis as *Impondoyendhlovu*, the horn of the elephant, because of its resemblance to ivory. It burns with a tremendous heat, and campers have found their kettles melted down to a lump of metal upon returning to an unattended campfire. Early settlers used white Leadwood ash as a whitewash for their homes. In one such old Leadwood tree, I found, all at the same time, nests of the Cape Glossy Starling, Striped Kingfisher, Redbilled Woodhoopoe and Yellowthroated Sparrow.

A beautiful little country of mountain and valley, river and forest, grassland and bushveld, Swaziland has a wealth of lovely birds and animals, and is indeed a wildlife photographer's joy.

W.P. Stanford

Swazi Flora

The richness and variety of Swaziland's flora makes the country a place of great interest to the botanist and nature lover. There are over 6 000 plant species, which include some 2 600 different species of flowering plants, ferns, and fern allies. This great range is due largely to the wide differences in altitude.

Outstanding floral species include aloes, of which there are some 25 varieties, ranging from the largest tree species, *Aloe bainesii*, to *Zantedschia*, the so-called arum lilies, including a burgundy-coloured variety, *Zantedschia rehmanni*, which is thought to be peculiar to Swaziland. Orchids include several showy species, and there are a number of different varieties of begonia, amaryllis, and gladiolus.

Some of the most striking trees are the *Cussonias* (cabbage trees) of the Highveld, the crimson-flowered *Schotia brachypetala*, the scarlet-flowered *Erythrina lysistemon*, the yellow-flowered *Pterocarpus rotundifolius* and *Pterocarpus angolensis*, and some magnificent species of *Ficus*.

There are many different succulents and some striking epiphytic plants. Ferns include two tree-ferns and a large variety of small species, in and out of the forest. There are at least six species of that remarkable botanical phenomenon the cycad (including *Encephalartos paucidentatus* and *Encephalartos lebomboensis*), the most primitive living seed-bearing plant known, which has survived almost unchanged during the past 50 million years. As in South Africa, cycads are strictly protected by law in Swaziland, and heavy penalties are prescribed for illegal possession and exportation.

The Swazi Economy

Swaziland has a mixed economy with a distinct orientation towards private ownership of production and a relatively free play of market forces. The economy itself has experienced significant structural changes over the years since independence in 1968. By looking at these structural changes and the respective roles of the private and public sectors one can get a general picture of the nature of the Swazi economy.

Industrialisation and Rural Development

From a general perspective, the economy has shifted out of primary production (agriculture, forestry, and mining) into secondary production (manufacturing, construction, electricity, and water) and tertiary production (private and public sectors).

This shift in the composition of production reflects a diversification of the economy. In particular, the increase in the proportion of manufacturing reflects an increase in the degree of industrialisation. However, if one considers that much of the manufacturing industry is agro-based (for example, as in the sugar-refining, pulp-milling, fruit-canning and textile industries) then the degree of secondary production is low. It is important, therefore, to focus also on the promotion of non-agro-based industries (such as those involved in the production of steel products, radios, watches, bicycles, television sets, and heaters).

Because of the small size of the domestic economy, production by the large firms is export oriented. As a result, the share of exports in total production is quite high (it averaged 70 per cent in the 1980s). This accounts for one dimension of the openness of the economy. Other dimensions of openness are a high proportion of imports in total production (averaging 100 per cent in the 1980s); the employment of a significant proportion of local labour abroad (predominantly in South Africa); the existence of a significant pool of expatriate labour; and the dominance of foreign capital in the private sector.

Within the agricultural industry, there are two types of economic dualism. One of these is Swazi Nation Land (communally-owned agricultural land) versus Individual Tenure Farms (ITFs). The other is Rural Development Areas (RDAs) versus non-RDAs. The RDA programme was instituted in the early years of independence with the intention of raising agricultural productivity on Swazi Nation Land (SNL). This programme has been successful to the extent that SNL production has become more market oriented (as opposed to subsistence oriented), and the productivity gap between SNL and ITFs has been reduced over the post-independence era. For instance, the contribution of SNL to crop production in the country rose from an annual average of 15 per cent over the first half of the 1980s to 26 per cent over the second half. To the extent that SNL accommodates 63 per cent of the population, the RDA programme is a suitable vehicle for reducing poverty in Swaziland.

Private and Public Sectors

The success of Swaziland's developmental efforts depends a great deal on both the public and private sectors. The latter plays a leading role in production and employment because of the private enterprise nature of the economy. For instance, by the end of the 1980s three-quarters of wage employment was provided directly by the private sector. The total level of wage employment itself was well above 100 000. The active farm population on the other hand exceeded 255 000, but most of it did not receive a wage for its services — it merely shared in the output.

The public sector largely plays a guiding and supportive role. At the domestic level it provides not only the necessary socio-economic infrastructure (such as roads, telecommunications, electricity, education, and healthcare facilities) but also, mostly in partnership with the private sector, directly productive capital. Currently, the infrastructure is overstretched as a result of the relatively high pace of industrialisation.

At an international level, the public sector has helped in the creation and maintenance of trade links — with the Southern African Customs Union, the Southern African Development Coordination Conference, the Preferential Trade Area for Eastern and Southern Africa, and the Lome Treaty (between the European Economic Community and the African-Caribbean-Pacific Group).

The Swazi economy is market oriented in the sense of having limited price controls. These are intended to protect low-income households on both the production and consumption sides. For instance, on the production side there are legislated minimum wages covering a range of industries and controlled producer prices for maize and milk. On the consumption side there are price controls on essential products like bread, milk, and soft drinks. Other than these limited controls, market forces are generally allowed to operate freely.

The involvement of the public sector in the economy has steadily increased over the post-independence era. This is evidenced by the number of sectors the government has entered, the proportion of national income appropriated through taxes, the proportion of public expenditure to national expenditure, and the proportion of public to national employment. For instance, the proportion of public revenues to gross domestic product (GDP) rose from an annual average of 28 per cent over the first ten years of independence to 36 per cent over the last ten years. The proportion of public spending to GDP rose from 30 per cent to 43 per cent over the respective periods. The proportion of public to national employment rose from 22 per cent to 29 per cent.

Dr M.S. Matsebula

Bibliography

Barker, Dudley. *Swaziland.* Corona Library. London. 1965.

Kuper, Hilda. *The Swazi: A South African Kingdom.* Holt, Rinehart & Winston. New York. 1963.

Marwick, Brian. *The Swazi.* Frank Cass & Co. London. 1966.

Matsebula, James. *A History of Swaziland.* 2nd Ed. Longman. Cape Town. 1976.

Miller, Alistair. *Mamisa, the Swazi Warrior.* Shuter & Shooter. Pietermaritzburg.

Nxumalo, Sishayi. *Our Way of Life.* Mbabane.

O'Neil, Owen. *Adventures in Swaziland.* George Allen & Unwin. London. 1921.

Winchester-Gould, G.A. *The Guide to Swaziland.* 3rd Ed. Winchester Press. Johannesburg. 1978.